Mizlyrics Life "Quotes"

Tawana Beecham

ABOUT THE BOOK

ABOUT THE BOOK
Discover profound insights and
heartfelt wisdom in'
Mizlyrics's Life "Quotes'
With creativity and compassion,
this collection offers healing poetry
and poignant reflections, aiming to
uplift souls and inspire positive
change.

I

Dedication

To all my quote lovers, I hope you enjoy my phenomenal rare quote book.

I've enjoyed writing all my life whether it's a poem, quote or a song. I have been inspired by many icons like Angela Mayo, Hangs-ton Hughes along among many more icons . My quotes come from everyday life experiences that I share hoping to shed light and inspire many others on my journey.

ACKNOWLEDGMENTS

I can't express enough how grateful I am to my family and friends who supported me throughout my journey by providing suggestions, personal input, thoughts, and feedback on my first professionally published book. My family and friends are the reason these brave quotes became reality, embracing the good with the bad.
I truly appreciate each and every one of these individuals for remaining consistent with me on my book-writing journey. I was also inspired by a writer named Peach McIntyre, whom I follow on social media.
She is a prolific content creator who radiates positivity and does not sugarcoat anything to make her situation look good for her viewers. McIntyre shares her experiences, whether good or bad, that have helped others along the way on their journey to success. She never allowed anything to get in her way of her greatness regardless of any struggles she faced throughout her life.

Andrew M Tuircuit Jr.
Ki'esha Beecham
Damon Wilson
Jasmine Beecham
Domanick McKinney –El
Peach Mcintyre

Contents

ABOUT THE BOOK..........................I
DEDICATION...............................II
ACKNOWLEDGEMENT III
ACKNOWLEDGEMENT.......................IV
INSPIRATIONAL QUOTES 5
LIFE QUOTES 13
RELATIONSHIP-QUOTES....................25
TROUBLED QUOTES 33
LOVE QUOTES 40
WORKPLACE QUOTES 43
MY THOUGHTS.................................. 50
SKETCH 61
JOURNAL - DAIRY 72

INSPIRATIONAL QUOTES

The key to success is
~consistency~

People will make you feel like
you can't because they can't.
Stay focused

Ecerything is a process
& giving up is never an option

5

Anything in life you desire is worth fighting for . Never give up

Stop doubting yourself because someone else doesn't believe in you .

Fear can hold you life back from many great opportunities

Absolutely no goal that you truly desire is too much to accomplish 🩶

Self-motivation is the realest verses depending on other-sources that are aren't guaranteed

If you carrying all the weight in relationship, you need a new title!

Not everyone has a strong mindset but never be negatively influenced by those who settle for less.

You're never too old to set goals for yourself

Everything is a process, it might take months even years giving up is never an option.

ANYTHING IS POSSIBLE WHEN YOU APPLY EFFORT.

Always surround yourself around people who want to see you win even if they haven't reached their goal.

Let negativity be your motivation to succeed unapologetically

People can be your biggest distraction
Focus on self-first, always!

You win by speaking the truth regardless
of who believes you.

Goals should always be a priority verses a
temporary distraction

Humbleness is appreciated more than
words could express.

Stay determined
& achieve everything
unapologetically

Be careful who you tell good
news. Sometimes it's always a but... Instead of
congratulations

Don't ever get discouraged when it comes
to accomplishing goals for yourself

People will make you feel like you can't
because they can't.
Stay focused

Sometimes it takes more than one job
to accomplish goals.
Never settle for less 💯

Situations do come about but
troubles don't last always

All is it takes is that one person
to believe in you . Your   life will
charge for the best forever. 🤍

Fulfill your purpose in life no matter how many
times you stumble.

Anything you desire in life is possible with consistent effort

Some situations will have you rethinking your whole life decisions. Strength is everything

Some folks loyalty is so fake, they never deserved your presence

Never stop being humble
because of selfish folks you
come in contact with

A person will take advantage of you then
play the victim. Let them swim their way out!

Peopleuocast ifbethappoymethfong they
can't accomplish!

Stop worrying what folks a think
Whether you do or don't they
still act the same .

When people use you, then
act ungrateful, that's selfish &
beyond personal!

People act like they so upset
with you when they really
dislike themselves .

SOME FOLKS ARE IMMUNE TO BEING TOXIC

People who been bullied their whole Child/ teen life, reflects that Energy on others as Adult

It's ok to do stuff for other folks but never put them before the ones who are priority in your life.

People will treat you different just
because you have a reserved
personality. Never change, ever.

Don't complain about so many
things in life .Make
wiser decisions for the better !Hh

Stop being so forgiving, unfortunately people
can be
selfish & greedy.

People can be your biggest
distraction. Focus on self-first,
always!

You win by speaking the truth
regardless of who believes
you.

Don't get discouraged accomplishing goals you set
for yourself .

Enjoy life & forgive those who
poured negativity (betrayal) in your
mix out of spite . remain humble

Manipulation is dangerous, it's
often used carelessly
out of spite

Some folks can't show gratitude for the
next due to lack of self achievements in
their life

YOU GET OUT OF LIFE WHAT
YOU POUR IN ~CHANGE IS
YOUR CHOICE ~

Your weakness becomes their
bait. Let them starve

Enjoy life & forgive those
whopoured negativity (betrayal)
in your heart out of envy.

FULFILL YOUR PURPOSE IN LIFE NO MATTER HOW MANY TIMES YOU STUMBLE!

The hardest decision to make can be the most beneficial to you forever.

Watch out for folks who get mad when you can do certain things better than them!

People will point out your flaws but won't acknowledge their own

Sometimes it take decades to accept a person for who they really are

Sometimes in life, people use you to survive not knowing they'll need you again.

It's a must you live life for self not to please others.

Some folks will purposely do say certain things just to
get a reaction.

Some folks can't be happy for you if it's not them

People will only tell the part that make
them look good
and you look bad

At some point a person have to grow up and
take control in their
life to be a successful individual.

Jealousy comes in disguise for
many reasons

The hardest decision to make can be the
most beneficial
to you forever.

Why complain when you
can change your situation
for the better.?

When a Taurus feels hurt or betrayed,
they will build a wall with no limits

You'll excuse all flaws in relationship until you're ready to accept facts ✓

Don't you make up excuses for
your mate because the
good overweigh the bad !

A women who makes   a manher
priority before herself is insecure

Some folks have adjusted themselves to accepting almost anything.

A women who makes   a man her priority before herself is insecure!

You'll excuse all flaws until you're ready to accept facts!

A women who makes a man her
priority before herself is insecure!

Some women will defend these men knowing
they need to better.

We all at some point settle for less but that's
definitely a choice

Don't waste your time on others who don't match your energy.

Avoid folks who only want to deal with you when it benefits them.

People do anything just to feel loved instead of valuing themselves more!

A person who got the opportunity to show appreciation but choose to be selfish is ignorant.

When an individual gets the opportunity to show their appreciation but act selfish.

A relationship is when two people come together, not one person carrying more weight.

When you make up excuses for your
mate because the good over
weighs the bad.

You'll excuse all flaws in a
relationship until you're ready to
accept facts.

The more you do the
less they'll appreciate anything

If you're carrying all the weight in a relationship you need a new title.

Relationships are overrated especially when it's not a two-way street

It's a choice to forgive disgusting folks who has wronged you & others that are closest to you!

Imagine living your life as if it couldn't change in a blink of eye.

Imagine needing the same person you didn't treat with respect.

A person will take advantage of you long as you allow it to go on ✓

SOME FOLKS MAKE YOU WISH YOU
WOULD HAVE MADE DIFFERENT CHOICES
IN LIFE

Manipulators users, liars, and NARCISSISTS are
worst people hto come in contact with!

People who do stuff for you because you did it
first don't have the
best intentions .

When you find a pure mate,
hold on to them and grow toogether 🩶

If you carrying all the weight in a
relationship , you need a new
title!

Some   Situations   will   have   you
rethinking your whole life decisions 🫤

When you make up excuses for your
mate because good over weighs the bad

Watch out for folks who get mad when
you can do something better than them

Relationships are overrated especially
when it's not a two-way street !

TROUBLED QUOTES

An individual who has sympathy for someone who is suffering from their poor choices and is hard on a close relative is weird.

Nothing excuses a person's behavior no matter who they are.

Some folks choose to protect the wrong to uphold their image.

The more you do for a person, the less they'll appreciate you. Always put self-first!

be Some ungrateful folks and will selfish forever until a wakeup call arrives.

Folks secretly be envious of you but still need you privately

Silence can save you physically but
kills you mentally!! speak

When   you   have   asupport
system, it   offers
🤍hope

People will do you wrong and act
like you hurt them

Folks who will defend a stranger
before a close relative is dangerous... be
careful, that's personal .

People who defend the lies they tell are
dangerous humans 😬

Sometimes it take decades to realize a
person's demeanor was never in
your best interest.

Be careful who you associate with,
some folks never liked you
but benefited from you

It's a choice to forgive certain folks who has wronged you & others that are closest to you.

People who have been bullied their whole child /teen life reflects that energy on others as an adult.

Imagine doing for someone who never compromises making it about them.

It's always the ones who can't compete that has the most to say.

If only life was predictable We'd make wiser choices.

When you treat someone with worth
they become selfish, ignorant &
ungrateful.

People will tell you a lie knowing
you know they're lying!

Stay away from people who can tell a LIE
and defend it
once CONFRONTED

Never put yourself in an uncomfortable
situation for another
person out of fear ✓

Sometimes you got to be responsible
enough to figure things out on your own !

It's easy to make excuses verses beneficial
to make progress 💯

Watch out for folks who get mad
when you can do something
better than them

One wrong decision doesn't mean your
life os over. ~keep faith~

Live in the moment with that special
someome who makes your heart happy

Love is a decision of commitment to share good & bad moments with that 1 person who accepts you unconditionally.

Find happiness with someone who appreciates your greatness while embracing your flaws

Intimacy is something shared between two people very patiently

Love is a gentle, bitter sweet
unforgettable feeling

Love can be blind when you
desperately desire companionship
💕

Love is a special feeling that gently
warms your heart in many ways!

Love can be confusing, deceiving or just pleasure at the moment

Love is mysteriously captivating and unpredictable in many aspects

A broken heart is capable of mending but sometimes the pain can feel like forever.

Love doesn't come with instructions.
You just grow on the journey .

Love is a amazing feeling when it's
with the right one

Love is unpredictable, it could creep
up on you unexpectedly💕

When training a new employee Don't enforce a rule that you dont with other employees old or new.

It will always be some type of discrepancy at the work place. Ignore ignorance & always speak out

Employers should always act professional treating all employee's equal ✓

Respect and professionalism
should be mandatory in the
workplace.

Don't let an unfortunate situation
of wrongfully terminated define
who you are.

WORKPLACE, HARASSMENT,
DISCRIMINATION, & BULLYING NEEDS TO
END 🩶

Unfortunately, 90% of workplace harassment is never officially reported. l

When someone has a position of authority it should be used correctly and truthfully to resolve issues in the workplace.

Employees should always feel comfortable to talk to their superiors at any time to resolve any issues.

Your voice has power , never
let anyone silence you at work or
any situation.

Never be afraid to speak up against
anyone who is making you feel
uncomfortable in the workplace

Diversity doesn't change these are all equal in
this world.

When someone has a position of authority
it should be used
correctly in the workplace

Professionalism is a must . Complaints should
always be enforced in the workplace 💯

Positive energy is important in
the workplace especially
when you hold a higher position.

It's important to feel safe and heard in
the work place !

Always stay focused and never
be afraid to tell someone when
you're   uncomfortable   in   the
workplace!

Avoid toxic situations in the workplace.
Always be respectful &
never accept disrespect 💯

My Thoughts

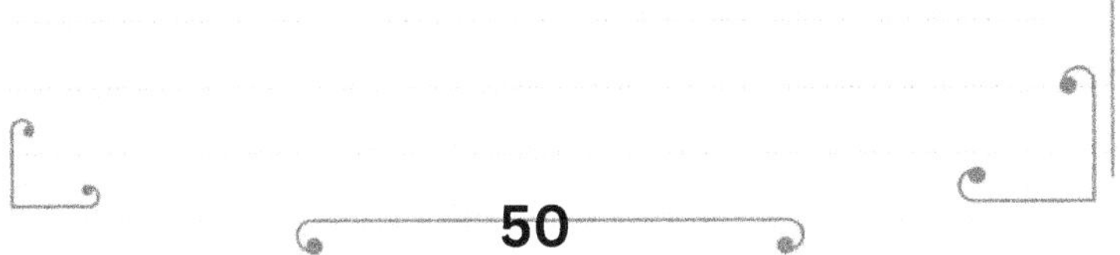

My Thoughts

My Thoughts

My Thoughts

My Thoughts

My Thoughts

My Thoughts

My Thoughts

My Thoughts

My Thoughts

Sketch

Sketch

Sketch

Sketch

Sketch

Sketch

Sketch

Sketch

Sketch

Sketch

Journal/Diary

Journal/Diary

Journal/Diary

Journal/Diary

Journal/Diary

Journal/Diary

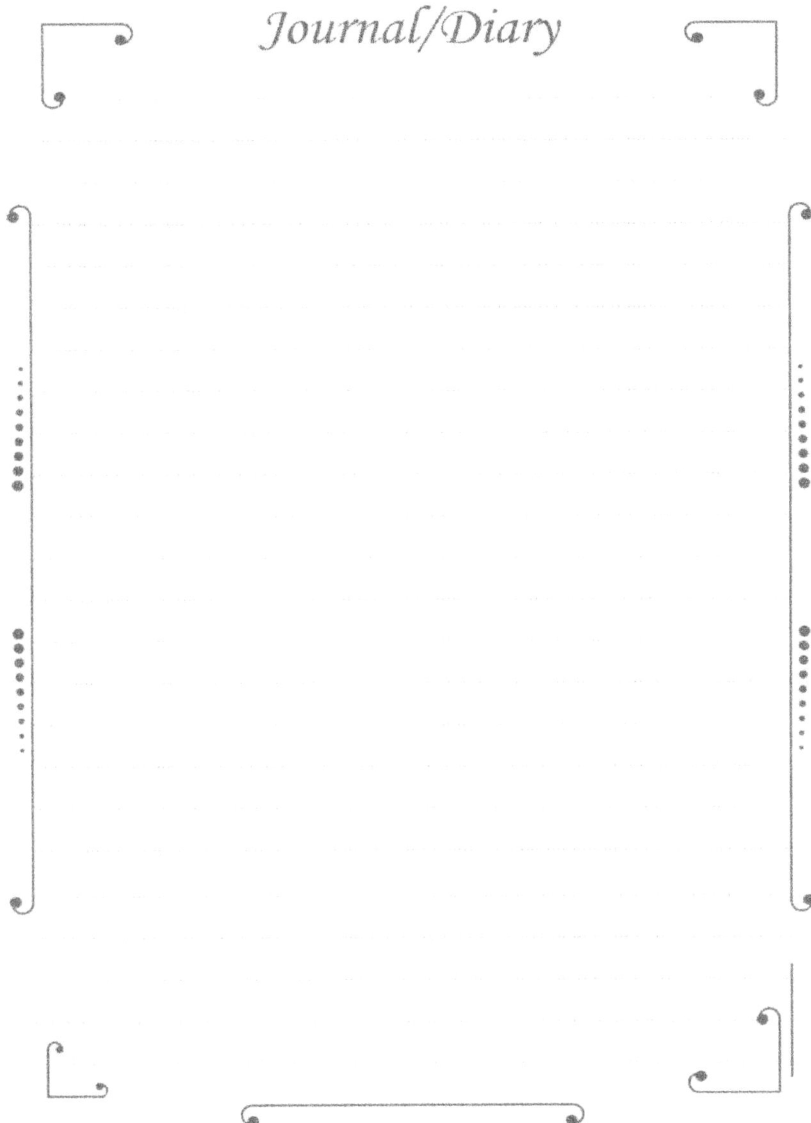

Journal/Diary

Journal/Diary

Journal/Diary

www.ingramcontent.com/pod-product-compliance
Lightning Source LLC
Chambersburg PA
CBHW040155160726
48006CB00014B/1761